PRAYERS
for Children

Elizabeth Laird
pictures by Margaret Tempest

COLLINS

For Jessica

William Collins Sons & Co Ltd
London · Glasgow · Sydney · Auckland
Toronto · Johannesburg

First published 1987
Second impression 1987
© text Elizabeth Laird 1987
© illustrations the Estate of Margaret Tempest 1987

British Library Cataloguing in Publication Data

Laird, Elizabeth
  Prayers for children.
  1. Children — Prayer books and devotions
  — English
  I. Title   II. Tempest, Margaret
  242′.82   BV4870

ISBN 0–00–191137–6

Printed and bound in Belgium
by Henri Proost & CIE PVBA

Foreword

Some kinds of prayers are easy to say, and some are harder. We all know how to ask God for help when we're in trouble, but it's not easy to ask him to forgive us, and it's sometimes hard to remember to praise him for his greatness, or to thank him for his goodness to us.

The little prayers in this book will help you to pray. The pictures might help you too. They were painted many years ago by Margaret Tempest, a famous artist, whose work has been loved by generations of children.

God made the cowslips in the field
and the buds on the silver birch tree.
And God made me.

God loves the flowers and the trees he made
and all living things on land and sea.
And God loves me.

In Springtime we can see
new life growing out of old branches.
And at Easter we remember
how Jesus died and rose again.
Lord, may the bad things in us die away,
and may the good things live and grow.

Thank you, God,
for our friends the animals,
both wild and tame.
Help us to protect them,
and look after them
as you look after us.

Thank you, Lord
for the food we eat,
for the clothes we wear,
for the games we play.
Help us never to forget
those who have little food to eat,
and few clothes to wear,
and no strength for playing games.

Bless our friends, dear Lord,
both young and old, big and small.
Bless those who can run fast,
and even more,
bless those who cannot run at all.

The sea is yours, Lord,
and you made it,
and it was you who made the dry land.
We thank you for the excitement
of playing in the water,
and for the safety
of playing on the land.

Forgive us, dear Lord,
when we're cross and unkind.
Help us to say sorry.
And help us to forgive
those who are unkind to us.

How did you make the rainbow,
And what is beyond the sky?
Why did you make the sun so hot,
And what makes the clouds race by?
You are the Lord, the Creator.
Only you know how and why.

For paints and music and books to read
and toys to play with and friends to love
and warmth inside on snowy days
thank you Lord.

MARGARET TEMPEST

In the wintry snow and icy cold
give us hearts on fire with faith and joy.
Cold outside and warm within.

In the starlight dim of a winter sky
give us hearts alight with peace and love.
Dark outside and bright within.

Lord Jesus, you were once a baby
and you grew up to be a perfect man.
We want to do the things you taught us
and grow up to be like you.

Now it's time for bed
and I'm going to sleep
and I think of what's happened today.

A fight with a friend,
and a job left undone,
and my best kind of cake for tea.

Help me, O God, when tomorrow comes,
to put right what is wrong,
to take back what I said,
and to finish my work.
And thank you for your goodness to me.

Be a light in the dark for us,
dear Lord we pray,
and as we lie sleeping
keep evil away.